GIRL CODE

The Unspoken Rules of Real Womanhood & Sisterhood

ECLESIA HOLMES

PUBLISHED IN 2026 BY PEN TO PURPOSE PUBLISHING, LLC

ECLESIA'S HOLMES
LINCOLN PARK, MI 48146

FOR PERMISSION REQUESTS, WRITE TO THE AUTHOR AT:
PENTOPURPOSEPUBLISHINGLLC@GMAIL.COM

ISBN: 979-8-9951413-0-3

COVER DESIGN BY CARAMEL XPRESSIONS
PRINTED IN U.S.A

Table of Contents

DEDICATION

To my daughters,

May you never settle. May you always lead with wisdom, protect your peace, and know your worth without question.

You are not the love you have received, you are the love you carry.

And to every woman who still believes in real love, this is your reset.

This is your roadmap.
This is your reminder that wanting a sisterhood is not desperation, it's divine.

This book is for you.

The healed you.
The healing you.
The hopeful you.

LOVE,
Mom

The Birth of Girl Code

Girl Code was born out of heartbreak, hard lessons, and years of lived experience.

After countless friendships where I poured out love, energy, and loyalty, often without reciprocity. I came to a difficult realization that many women were never taught how to be a friend, because no one ever modeled it for them.

For a long time, I confused love with rescuing. I made saving people my role. What started as care slowly turned into entitlement, emotional exhaustion, and grief. I mourned friendships that drained me more than they fed me.

Still, I carry no bitterness. I love every woman I've had to disconnect from. I pray for them. I wish them peace and growth. But the truth is, we did not align. And alignment matters.

Out of that grief came clarity.

Out of that clarity came boundaries.

And out of those boundaries came Girl Code.

This book is the result of years of mistakes, healing, and revelation. It is for every woman who has:

- Struggled to find safe sisterhood
- Wanted deeper friendships without losing herself
- Loved hard, stayed too long, or overextended in the name of loyalty
- Desired community, but needed wisdom to protect her heart

Girl Code is not about perfection.

It is about presence, accountability, healing, and legacy.
It is a guide for women who want to build friendships rooted in trust, not trauma. Connection, not competition. And sisterhood that is sacred, not performative.

For Those Who Never Had A Circle

This book isn't just about friendships gone wrong. The book is about the pain we carry from the very women who were supposed to protect us. It's the betrayal that came with a smile. The competition we never asked for. The judgment sounded like concern. The silence that hurt more than words. We need this book because our circles weren't always sacred. Some of them were toxic, abusive, or performative; rooted in pain, jealousy, and unhealed trauma. Our families carried wounds they never healed, then passed those wounds on as an inheritance. In our careers and workplaces, we've been overlooked, underpaid, and undermined sometimes by other women who looked just like us. In our communities, too many women operate in a state of survival, mistaking defense for discernment and shade for strength. We need this book because we are not well, and no one's checking on us unless we fall apart.

This book is a mirror and a map. A mirror that shows us the parts of ourselves we've hidden or hardened. A map that guides us back to healthy womanhood, honest sisterhood, and healing that actually sticks. The Lack of Mentorship, Modeling, and Safe Spaces. You were never "too sensitive", you were just never given a space where sensitivity was safe. You weren't "too needy"; you were trying to survive around women who didn't know how to pour.

We didn't have enough:

Mothers who affirmed us.
Aunts who protected us.
Cousins who celebrated us.
Coworkers who uplifted us.
Friends who were loyal without conditions.

What we had instead were:

Women who are projected on instead of being nurtured.
Silent treatment is a form of verbal and emotional weaponry.
Passive-aggressive rivalries in family group chats.
Cliques in churches and cattiness at jobs.

But now, we break the cycle.

WHAT SISTERHOOD IS NOT

Sisterhood is NOT:

Being loyal to dysfunction because "that's still your family."
Bonding over gossip and pretending it's "venting."
Calling someone sis while secretly hating on her.
Using silence or shame as control.
Tolerating harmful behavior because it came from another woman.

Real sisterhood doesn't guilt you for growing. It doesn't shrink when you shine. It doesn't envy your freedom or mock your healing.

A LETTER TO THE READER:

"You are not hard to love, your circle just wasn't sacred."

Sis, maybe your first heartbreak wasn't romantic; it was maternal. Maybe your first betrayal came from your own last name. Perhaps you don't trust women, and with what you've seen, that's understandable. But let me say this with love and clarity: You were never the problem. You were just in rooms that never saw your worth. You were encouraged in environments that taught you to be strong, not soft. You have shown up for everyone, but everyone seems to disappear or doesn't prioritize you when it's their turn to show up.

This book is for you.

For the women with big hearts and no safety net. For the ones healing from both their enemies and their elders. For the ones craving sisterhood but terrified of being hurt again.

You are not alone anymore. You are not dramatic. You aren't broken beyond repair. You're just overdue for a new circle. You're just overdue for a new circle.

Welcome home.

CHAPTER 1

CODE OF PRESENCE: BE WHERE YOU SAY YOU ARE

The Rule: Don't flake on your sisters, emotionally or physically.

WHAT THIS REALLY MEANS:

Presence is more than physical attendance. It's emotional availability, spiritual alignment, and intentional communication.

We all move through different seasons of life.

Some are healing. Some are raising children. Some are working double shifts. Some are overwhelmed. And that's understood, but no matter the season, sisterhood still deserves effort.

WHEN YOU CAN'T SHOW UP, COMMUNICATE.

Nobody expects perfection, but silence can feel like abandonment, especially for women who have experienced abrupt departures with little or no explanation before. This isn't just a friendship. It's a relationship. A covenant. A covering.

Say something. Don't disappear. Acknowledge her value. Reevaluate. Make time. Repair the moment. "Sometimes it's not the absence that breaks us. It's the lack of care that followed."

ALL COMMUNICATION AIN'T A CALL

Let's be real: we don't always have time to talk. But presence doesn't require paragraphs.

It could look like:

- A simple "Thinking of you" text
- A funny meme she'd love
- A voice note: "I miss you. We're overdue."
- Tagging her in a memory or photo
- Sending a prayer her way and letting her know you did

Because this relationship is like no other. It is layered, sacred, and spiritual. You don't have to spend hours talking. You can have 8 seconds to remind her she matters.

BALANCE IS KEY

Everyone has different responsibilities.

Some have kids, others don't.
Some have more freedom, others have heavier loads.

So no, we don't always need to "match energy", but we do need to match intention. Effort. Care. Heart.

MAKE IT RIGHT

If you've been absent, be honest about where you've been. Reach out without shame. Offer a time to reconnect, intentionally. Make her feel like a priority, not an afterthought.

SCRIPTURE

"Never abandon a friend, either yours or your father's. When disaster strikes, you won't have to ask your brother for assistance. It's better to go to a neighbor than to a brother who lives far away."

Proverbs 27:10 (NLT)

When I'm unavailable, do I still find ways to be present in small moments?

____

____

____

Have I communicated my own capacity clearly to the women I love?

____

____

____

Who in my life has shown up for me recently, and have I thanked them?

____

____

____

Do I give the kind of support I desire?

____

____

____

Are there conversations or connections I need to revisit with honesty?

____

____

____

HEALING QUESTIONS
FOR THE ONES WHO WERE LEFT HANGING

What did presence look like in my childhood home?

____

____

____

Who didn't show up for me, and what did that teach me about my worth?

____

____

____

Do I expect people to disappear? If so, why?

Have I started isolating to protect myself from disappointment?

Am I open to rebuilding connections with people who tried even imperfectly?

What would it look like to trust that I'm safe now?

How can I reintroduce safe sisterhood into my life without fear?

God doesn't ghost.

He is the same yesterday, today, and forever. Let His consistency be your compass. Be the friend you prayed for. Be the sister you needed. Be where you say you are. Presence isn't about perfection. It's about priority.

CHAPTER 2:

CODE OF CELEBRATION: CLAP LOUDLY & GENUINELY

The Rule: Don't compete where you could collaborate.

THE HEART OF THIS CODE

This code serves as a reminder that another woman's success is not a loss for you. It's not subtraction, it's multiplication.

In our world, we were often taught to be suspicious of one another. Love is limited, and support is scarce. Many of us learned to compete instead of connect. But sisterhood isn't survival of the fittest. It's a circle of women choosing faith over fear, cheering over comparing, and lifting over looking down. We don't celebrate because we've arrived. We celebrate because we're committed to staying whole even while we're still waiting.

HOOD POPULARITY VS. REAL SUPPORT

Let's be real: in too many communities, supporting women typically meant supporting those who are loud, visible, or already winning. Support that comes in this form is not sisterhood, it's performance. Let's define the difference.

Hood Popularity:

Based on image, cliques, or status
Only shows up when it's trending
Attached to performance or aesthetic
Public praise but no private check-in
Hood popularity claps when it's convenient.

Real Support:

Based on love, effort, and real presence
Shows up even when it's quiet or hard
Attached to purpose, healing, and growth
Private check-in and public celebration
Real sisterhood claps because of its conviction.

WHEN DO WE CLAP?

We clap for the wins that society celebrates, but we also clap for the ones that go unnoticed.

You clap when your sister:
Buys a car
Gets the job
Starts therapy
Leaves a toxic relationship
Raises her kids alone
Rents or buys a house
Pays off a credit card
Goes back to school
Gets engaged
Joins a church, book club, or business
Learns how to rest and say "no" without guilt
Survives a hard day with grace

Sometimes those "I did it!" texts aren't just updates; they're her asking, "Can you see me? Can you clap for me?"

WHY IT CAN BE HARD TO CLAP

Jealousy and comparison don't make you a bad person. They make you human, and often, unhealed.

We struggle to celebrate others sometimes when:

We doubt ourselves.
We feel like we're behind.
We believe in scarcity instead of abundance.
We learned to compete for male attention, the spotlight, and love.
We never saw women genuinely celebrate each other growing up.

REFLECTION PROMPTS
WHY CAN'T I CLAP?

Sometimes, the root isn't in what she did, it's in what you haven't healed. Sit with these questions and be honest with yourself:

- Do I secretly believe that another woman's win means there's less left for me?

- Where in my life do I feel behind, and how is that showing up in my attitude toward others?

- Was I raised to see other women as competition or community?

- What was the first moment I remember feeling like another girl got chosen over me?

Do I feel like I'm enough, or do I still think I have to earn love, status, or worth?"

____

____

When a woman around me wins, do I compare or clap? Why?

____

____

Have I ever seen women in my life genuinely celebrate each other, or was it fake love, shade, and silence?

____

____

Healing begins when honesty takes precedence.

TOOLS TO HEAL & CELEBRATE GENUINELY

Root your identity in self-worth, not hierarchy.

Her winning does not mean you're losing. Her fostering a relationship with God doesn't mean you're forgotten; your relationship with God is staggering.

Practice private celebration.

Support isn't always a repost. It's a voice note, a surprise lunch, or a quiet, "I see you, sis."

Acknowledge envy without shame.

Try journaling: "Heal that place in me so I can clap genuinely."

Train your spirit: One clap a day. Set an intention to clap for one woman every day, whether in person, online, or in your heart. Start there.

THE ROLE OF EMPATHY AND COMPASSION

True celebration cannot exist without empathy and compassion.

Let's break those down:

Empathy is feeling with someone, not just for them. It's choosing to sit in her story, instead of judging it. "I may not understand everything you're going through, but I'm with you." Empathy is connection over correction.

Compassion is empathy with legs. It doesn't just say "I feel you," it shows up for you. "You won? Let me repost." "You lost? Let me check in." "You're tired? Let me offer space or help." Compassion is not pity.

Its presence. It's sacred support, not performance.

SCRIPTURE

"Pay careful attention to your own work, for then you will get the satisfaction of a job well done, and you won't need to compare yourself to anyone else."

Galatians 6:4 NLT

If your claps are quiet because your wounds are loud, take your time, but don't stay silent forever. The next time your sister wins, choose to clap anyway.

CHAPTER 3:

CODE OF CONFIDENTIALITY: WHAT WE SHARE STAYS HERE

The Rule: Sacred conversations don't leave the room, unless you've been given permission or you're taking it to God.

THE SAFEKEEPERS

The women who want to be trusted and who are trusted well. Because nothing weakens sisterhood faster than a loose tongue.

WHAT IS GOSSIP?

Gossip is sharing someone's personal business without consent, whether it's for entertainment, judgment, bonding, or attention. Even when it's labeled as "just venting," if the story isn't yours to tell and it doesn't serve a higher purpose, it's still gossip. Intent matters. But impact matters more.

"A gossip betrays a confidence, but a trustworthy person keeps a secret."

Proverbs 11:13

GOSSIP VS. NON-GOSSIP

Non-Gossip

- "She told me in confidence. I'm not repeating it."
- "Let's pray for her without sharing details."
- "Can I ask her permission to involve someone who could help?"

Gossip

- "She told me not to tell anyone, but I trust you."
- "She's back with him again; she never learns."
- "I know what's really going on with her. She fronts online."

If it shrinks her dignity, it's not love. If it entertains you at her expense, it's not sisterhood.

WHAT SHOULD BE KEPT SACRED?

Before you speak about someone else, ask yourself:

- Did she say this publicly?
- Was this shared in a vulnerable moment?
- Would she be embarrassed if others knew?
- Would I want this said about me?

Some things are always sacred:

- Trauma
- Mental health struggles
- Relationship or marriage challenges
- Parenting decisions
- Financial hardship
- Any situation she's still processing

If you're unsure, don't say it. Take it to God. Write it in your journal. Process it with a therapist. Protecting someone else's story also protects your spirit.

THE FRIEND-GROUP MISCONCEPTION

Just because you're in the same circle doesn't mean you share the same access. Every woman holds different levels of trust with different people.

Assuming "everyone already knows" can:

- Expose your friend
- Damage her safety
- Destroy the trust she placed in you

If she didn't say it to everyone, please don't make it known.

PILLOW TALK IS NOT PERMISSION

Yes, you love your partner. Yes, intimacy involves communication. But your friend's story does not belong in your bed.

Why it matters:

- Your partner doesn't carry the same grace for her that you do
- Opinions formed privately can damage relationships publicly
- Oversharing teaches that your circle isn't sacred

You can be deeply connected to your partner and deeply loyal to your sister. Those two things can coexist.

WHEN FRIENDSHIP ENDS OR BECOMES PAINFUL

Sometimes friendships don't just fade; they fracture. A former friend can begin to feel like an emotional opponent. The temptation is to unload what she once trusted you with. But don't.

How you handle her secrets after the relationship ends reveals your character, not hers.

What to do instead:

- Journal honestly
- Pray through the grief
- Talk to a therapist
- Heal without betraying sacred moments

You don't have to destroy what you once helped build just because the relationship changed.

EMOTIONAL SAFETY IS A SISTERHOOD STANDARD

Sisterhood should feel like:

- A vault
- A sanctuary
- A place where healing happens without fear of exposure

If she opens up and later feels embarrassed, the issue isn't vulnerability; it's a breach. A safe woman is a gift.

I may no longer be your friend, but I'm still your keeper.

If I ever loved you, your story is still safe with me.

That is integrity.
That is maturity.
That is Girl Code.

REFLECTION PROMPTS

Who taught me to gossip, and what did it cost me?

____

____

Have I ever broken someone's trust by sharing their story?

____

How do I process friendship loss without using secrets as ammunition?

____

____

How would I feel if my most painful moments were shared during a fallout?

Do I trust myself to be a safe space, and do others trust me?

"I may no longer be your friend, but I'm still your keeper." If I ever loved you, your story is still safe with me. That is integrity. That is maturity.

That is Girl Code.

CHAPTER 4:

CODE OF GROWTH: ACCOUNTABILITY WITHOUT SHAME

The Rule: Correct with care. Growth should never come through humiliation.

THE HEART OF THIS CODE

Growth does not happen in echo chambers. It happens in relationships where truth can be spoken safely.

But here's the part we often forget: Truth without tenderness can feel like betrayal.

We are not helping our sisters grow if we stay silent out of fear or pretend everything is fine. At the same time, we are not helping if we deliver correction with sarcasm, shade, or superiority. Correction is not condemnation. It is care.

Real sisterhood means we are willing to lovingly pull one another aside and say: "Friend, I care about you too much not to say something."

WHY IT'S HARD TO CORRECT OUR FRIENDS

Many women struggle with accountability in friendships because:

- We don't want to seem judgmental.
- We're afraid of hurting her feelings.
- We know she's been through a lot.
- We fear she might take offense or pull away.
- We're still working through our own growth, too.

But friendship is not a silent agreement. It is a sacred responsibility. The same way we hope someone would lovingly correct us, we owe that same honesty to our sisters.

HOW TO CORRECT A FRIEND WITH COMPASSION

1. Start with softness, not sarcasm.

Set the tone with love. Tone matters as much as truth.

Instead of: "Girl, you sounded ridiculous saying that."
Try: "Friend, I love you. Can I offer another perspective?"

2. Correct in private, not in public.

Public correction often leads to embarrassment and defensiveness. Private correction feels like protection. If the goal is growth, the conversation should feel safe, not exposing.

3. Avoid shaming, try explaining instead. Accountability should invite reflection, not humiliation.

Shame says: "You're wrong and you should feel bad."
Growth says: "I see it differently, and I want to share why."

4. Offer alternatives

Don't just point out what was wrong; offer a better way. Guidance helps growth become practical.

For example:
"Maybe next time you could say it this way..."

SOMETIMES DELIVERY MATTERS MORE THAN INTENTION

Sometimes the message is right, but the delivery blocks the lesson. Many of us have had to learn this the hard way. It's easy to lead with emotion instead of intention.

Instead, lead with:

- Understanding
- Clarity
- Patience

Ask yourself: If the roles were reversed, how would I want to be corrected? Speak to your friend the way you would hope to be spoken to.

IT'S ALSO OKAY TO TEACH

Correction without guidance can leave people feeling lost. The truth is, many women were never taught certain emotional or relational skills. Sisterhood sometimes means filling in the gaps.

You might help her learn:

- How to apologize and take accountability
- How to regulate emotions during conflict
- How to move out of survival mode and toward healing
- How to shift limiting or toxic thinking patterns

Don't just flag the mistake. Walk with her through the lesson. You're not just pointing something out, you're helping her grow.

HOW SHE RECEIVES IT... IS HER RESPONSIBILITY

Speak gently. Speak clearly. Say it once, maybe twice. After that, how she responds is up to her.

If she becomes defensive, that's human.
If she lashes out, it may be projection.
If she continues the same behavior after an honest conversation, that becomes a choice.
And that is where your boundaries come in.

WHEN GROWTH BECOMES A DEAL BREAKER

If a friend consistently:

- Dismisses your concerns
- Refuses to reflect on her actions
- Blames everyone else
- Rejects accountability entirely

...it may be time to reassess the relationship.

Ask yourself:

- Can I be honest here without shrinking?
- Is this friendship mutual or emotional labor?
- Am I allowed to grow here, too?

Healthy friendships allow space for both truth and transformation. Accountability is a love language.

Real sisterhood does more than point out mistakes. It teaches. It encourages. It stretches us toward better.

You are not just her friend. You are her mirror. Her reminder. Her safe push forward.

True sisterhood requires us to:

- Correct privately
- Speak gently
- Push with purpose
- Teach with patience

Because when women challenge each other in love, we rise together.

REFLECTION & JOURNAL PROMPTS

When was the last time I corrected a friend with love?

____

____

How do I usually respond when I'm the one being corrected?

____

____

Do I give my friends room to grow, or do I expect perfection?

____

What are my dealbreakers when a friend refuses accountability?

____

____

Am I truly a safe space for honest conversations?

SCRIPTURE

"Wounds from a sincere friend are better than many kisses from an enemy."

Proverbs 27:6

CHAPTER 5:

CODE OF GRACE: WE DON'T CANCEL, WE CONFRONT

The Rule: Address the issue with honesty before you walk away.

LET'S BE REAL

This chapter is personal. For a long time, I confused peace with detachment. When I felt hurt or offended, I went quiet. Not because I didn't care, but because I cared too much. My words could be sharp, my heart was sensitive, and confrontation felt like a battlefield. So silence became my protection.

But growth taught me something important:

Healing requires hard conversations. Avoidance doesn't protect your peace; it only postpones the pain.

EMOTIONAL MATURITY VS. EMOTIONAL ABANDONMENT

Emotional Maturity

- "That hurt me. Can we talk about it?"
- Creates clarity
- Offers grace
- Invites accountability

Emotional Abandonment

- "That hurt me, so I'm done with you."
- Leaves confusion
- Creates distance without explanation

- Holds onto resentment

This code isn't about letting people mistreat you. It's about allowing someone to be accountable before you walk away. You don't have to cancel her. You can confront her with clarity, compassion, and care.

THE GRACE PERIOD: Allowing space for self-correction.

One practice that changed my relationships is this: Before confronting someone, I pause. I observe. I give space. I wait to see if they recognize the issue themselves. Sometimes people do. And when they don't, that also tells you something.

But grace has an expiration date. Grace is patient, not passive. When silence turns into avoidance, it's time to have the conversation.

RESPECT: THE ROOT OF HEALTHY CONFRONTATION

Let's name what's often underneath the hurt. Most of the time, the issue isn't just pain, it's disrespect.

Respect means honoring someone's:

- feelings
- time
- boundaries
- presence

Disrespect doesn't always arrive loudly. Sometimes it shows up as:

- dismissal
- avoidance
- subtle comments
- a shift in energy

When you confront someone about disrespect, you're not trying to humble them. You're honoring yourself.

And that requires:

- Time to cool down.
- Empathy to consider their wounds.
- Compassion is not to match negative energy.
- Grace to leave the conversation with dignity.

MY PERSONAL SHIFT

I had to unlearn silence as a defense mechanism. I had to learn to speak before frustration turned into distance. I had to practice saying what I felt, even if the conversation didn't fix everything. Because now, when I leave a situation, I leave with clarity instead of confusion. I give people space. I listen for accountability. But when I'm met with deflection, dishonesty, or avoidance? I remind myself that someone's inability to take responsibility says more about their healing than my worth. And sometimes the most peaceful response is simply stepping away with compassion.

HARD CONVERSATIONS CAN HEAL

You may not always get closure. But you can gain clarity, and clarity is powerful. Sometimes confrontation restores the relationship. Sometimes it reveals that the relationship has run its course. Both outcomes still move you forward.

- Do I give people space to correct themselves before confronting them?

- Have I ever ghosted someone who didn't know what they did wrong?

- What does disrespect look like to me?

- Do I feel safe enough to say, "That hurt me"?

- What scares me more: confrontation or being misunderstood?

REFLECTION PROMPTS

Describe a time someone gave you grace. How did it affect you?

____

____

Think about a time you avoided a difficult conversation. What held you back?

____

____

Recall a moment when you felt deeply disrespected. How did you respond then, and how would you respond now?

____

____

____

Write a conversation starter you could use in the future: "I value our relationship, but something has been weighing on me. Can we talk about it?"

____

____

____

____

____

SCRIPTURE

"If your brother or sister sins, go and point out their fault, just between the two of you."

Matthew 18:15

Scripture doesn't teach us to gossip, ghost, or retaliate.
It teaches us to go directly to the person with honesty and grace.

You don't have to explode. You don't have to disappear. You don't have to match the energy that hurt you. You can confront with compassion. You can speak with self-respect. You can check someone without canceling them.

And if they still refuse to honor the relationship? Leave with peace. Not confusion. Not chaos. Not bitterness. Because that is the Code of Grace. We don't ghost.

We give space, speak truth, and move forward when necessary.

CHAPTER 6:

CODE OF IDENTITY: HER SHINE DOESN'T DULL YOURS

THE RULE: You don't have to dim her light to feel seen.

You were never called to be a copy. Your lane, your purpose, and your timing are divinely designed.

THE REAL

It's hard to celebrate others when your own life feels chaotic. It's hard to show up for your sister when you haven't shown up for yourself. When we lose connection with our own identity, insecurity can creep in. And when insecurity grows, it often spills out in subtle ways, through jokes, silence, sarcasm, or side-eyes. That kind of energy can quietly damage what was meant to be sacred. A lack of identity often turns into projection.

IDENTITY VS. INSECURITY

You may be losing sight of yourself when:

- You struggle to celebrate unless you're in the spotlight too
- Your jokes carry hidden resentment
- You smile outwardly but quietly wonder, "Why not me?"

Let's be clear. Those feelings don't make you a bad person. They make you human. But it is your responsibility to recognize those emotions and address them with honesty. Healing begins with awareness.

THE DANGER OF MISPLACED FEELINGS

When we're emotionally or spiritually drained, we may unintentionally project our frustrations onto others.

Sometimes it sounds like:

- "Must be nice."
- "I see she forgot about her day ones."
- "She's doing too much now."

These comments may feel like jokes in the moment. But they land like daggers. They can humiliate someone who trusted you and reveal deeper feelings that need healing.

WHAT IT LOOKS LIKE VS. WHAT IT FEELS LIKE

What Was Said	What It May Signal	How It Can Feel to Her
"Oh, she's acting brand new."	Feeling abandoned or left behind	Like she's being punished for growing
"She's on her high horse now."	Insecurity about personal progress	Like she has to shrink to stay accepted
"Let's see how long it lasts."	Expecting her failure	Like her success isn't believed

Words matter. Energy matters even more.

WHEN TO PULL BACK AND RECALIBRATE

Sometimes the most loving thing you can do is pause. If your heart isn't in the right place, don't force a fake celebration.

Instead: Talk to God.

"Lord, help me clean out the parts of me that are comparing, competing, or craving attention."

Be honest with yourself. "Am I inspired or intimidated?" Growth begins where honesty lives.

KEEPING JEALOUSY OUT OF THE CIRCLE

Healthy sisterhood requires intentional work. Here are a few ways to protect your friendships from comparison:

1. Pray over your circle. Not just for success, but for healed hearts, healthy motives, and unity.

2. Be honest when you're struggling. It's okay to say: "Sis, I'm proud of you. I'm just working through some things in my own life right now."

3. Celebrate out loud. Private support is beautiful. Public support is powerful.

4. Stay in your lane. Purpose doesn't compete, it complements.

5. Confess envy before it grows. Bring it to God before it becomes gossip, distance, or resentment.

"For where you have envy and selfish ambition, there you find disorder and every evil practice."

James 3:16 (NIV)

Where jealousy grows, peace disappears. Where comparison lives, connection struggles to survive. True sisterhood cannot thrive on silent shade or fake support.

REFLECTION QUESTIONS

Am I truly proud of her, or do I sometimes feel left behind?

____

Have I ever made someone's moment about my own insecurities?

____

If a friend told me she felt unsupported by me, would I feel surprised or convicted?

____

PRAYER

God, heal every part of me that feels unseen, small, or insecure. Remind me that I am fearfully and wonderfully made. Help me celebrate others without comparison, support without shade, and show up in my friendships as whole, healed, and grounded in You. Amen.

Her win is not your loss. Her light doesn't dim yours; it simply reveals where you still need to reconnect with your own power and purpose. Stay plugged into who you are. Because when women are secure in their identity, sisterhood becomes stronger, not competitive.

CHAPTER 7:

CODE OF BOUNDARIES: LOVE WITHOUT OVERGIVING

The Rule: Love shouldn't deplete you.

LET'S START HERE

You were never called to bleed for the people you were meant to bless. You can love someone deeply and still say no. You can be her safe space without becoming her entire shelter. Because real love does not require you to lose yourself in order to help someone else. Healthy sisterhood allows both women to grow, not one to carry the other.

DEFINITIONS THAT MATTER

Understanding these dynamics helps protect both you and your friendships.

Boundaries: Healthy protective lines that keep your peace sacred. They define where you end, and someone else begins.

People-Pleasing: When you betray your own needs to gain approval. This is often rooted in fear, not love.

Codependency: An emotional reliance on being needed. You begin to feel responsible for how others think, live, or function.

Savior Complex: The belief that it's your job to rescue everyone. But you are not her God, healer, or miracle worker. You are her friend.

WHAT THIS LOOKS LIKE IN REAL LIFE

Many women love their sisters fiercely. We cry together. We pray together. We stretch for one another. We don't want to see the women we love struggle. But sometimes our help becomes their handicap. Sisterhood is not about carrying someone forever. It's about helping each other stand.

SUPPORT VS. OVERFUNCTIONING

Healthy sisterhood looks like sharing resources and wisdom.

You might exchange:

- recipes and Bible verses
- strategies and solutions
- savings tips and survival plans
- business ideas and financial goals

That is beautiful, but support has boundaries.

You can:

- Send her the instructions
- Share the resource
- Walk her through the process once
- Offer guidance and encouragement

But you should not:

- Fill out her paperwork
- Handle her responsibilities
- Speak to customer service on her behalf
- Call off work for her

- Become her emotional secretary or unpaid assistant

Because when you always do the work for someone, they never learn how to do it for themselves. You can lead her to the water, but you cannot swim it for her. That's not grace. That's enablement.

LET THE WORD GROUND YOU

"Let your 'Yes' be 'Yes,' and your 'No,' 'No.' Anything more comes from the evil one."

Matthew 5:37

Even Jesus rested. Even Jesus said no. Even Jesus withdrew from crowds to protect His peace. You are not weak for protecting your energy. You are wise for preserving it.

QUICK GUT CHECKS

Ask yourself honestly:

- Is she growing from my support or leaning on me as a crutch?
- Do I feel uplifted after our conversations or drained?
- Have I been saying yes out of guilt instead of love?

Boundaries often reveal what relationships truly depend on.

WORDS YOU ARE ALLOWED TO SAY

Without guilt.
Without apology.
Without explanation.

You can say:

- "Not today."
- "I don't have the capacity right now."
- "You've got this. I believe in you."
- "I can't carry this one, but I can pray with you."
- "Here's the link, sis. Let me know how it goes."

Healthy love empowers. It does not exhaust.

PRAYER

God, help me love with wisdom. Teach me how to give without draining myself. Show me where I have taken on burdens You never asked me to carry. Help me say no without guilt and love without losing myself. Remind me that boundaries do not block love; they protect it. And help my sister understand that when I rest, I am not abandoning her. I am preserving the strength You placed within me. Amen.

At first, I didn't understand.

When you stopped overextending yourself, I thought you stopped loving me.

But now I see something different.

You didn't withdraw your love; you changed how you showed it.

You stopped doing everything for me.

And you started teaching me how to stand on my own.

That's when I began to grow.

So thank you for the boundaries.

Thank you for the moments you said no.

Thank you for holding space without always holding me up.

I didn't understand it then.

But I respect it now.

You didn't stop loving me.

And sis... that may have saved me more than anything else ever could.

CHAPTER 8:

CODE OF EMOTIONAL INTELLIGENCE: DON'T WEAPONIZE HER
VULNERABILITY

The Rule: Her pain is not your ammunition.

Sisterhood isn't only about the joyful moments. It's about how we hold each other through the difficult ones. Sometimes a friend will trust you with the parts of herself she's ashamed of; the messy, painful, or confusing parts she doesn't show the world.

Emotional intelligence in friendship means handling those moments with care, even when you feel triggered, hurt, or confused. You are not responsible for fixing her life. But you are responsible for not deepening her wounds.

LET'S DEFINE SOMETHING IMPORTANT

Sometimes a friend shares what we might call her ugly truths. These are the raw, unfiltered confessions that come out in moments of honesty and vulnerability.

Examples might sound like:

- "I scream at my kids when I'm overwhelmed."
- "I keep choosing men who aren't good for me."
- "Some days I really don't like myself."
- "I push people away when they get close."
- "I feel like I'm barely holding it together."

These moments are not meant to be repeated. They are entrusted.

WHEN YOU HEAR THE HARD STUFF

There may be times when your friend says or does something that doesn't reflect the woman you know she truly is. Maybe she vents out of exhaustion. Maybe she reacts in frustration. Maybe she says something harsh in a moment of overwhelm. Your instinct might be to correct her immediately. But wisdom often requires patience. Sometimes the best response is to wait until emotions settle.

Then you approach her gently: "Friend, what's really going on? You sound overwhelmed. I know this moment doesn't reflect who you truly are."

You don't excuse harmful behavior. But you also don't shame someone who is already struggling. Instead, you offer a lifeline, a space where honesty can lead to healing.

THE POWER OF REFRAMING

Your role as a sister is not to tear her down. It is to redirect her with care.

Instead of saying: "You're toxic."
Try saying: "Sis, I know you're better than this moment. Let's talk about what's really going on."

Acknowledging someone's pain while guiding them toward growth creates space for transformation.

WHEN THE CONFESSIONS ARE HEAVY

Sometimes a friend will share struggles that feel far outside your own experience. She might talk about impulsive decisions, complicated relationships, or habits she feels ashamed of. In those moments, judgment closes doors. Curiosity opens them.

Instead of reacting, you might ask:

- "What do you think you're looking for when you make that choice?"
- "How do you usually feel afterward?"
- "What do you wish was different?"

You may not have the answers. And that's okay. Your job isn't to solve her life, it's to hold space while she processes it.

WHAT WEAPONIZING VULNERABILITY LOOKS LIKE

When friendships break down, there can be a temptation to throw someone's past pain back at them. But real sisters refuse to do that.

Weaponizing vulnerability sounds like:

- Bringing up past confessions during arguments
- Mocking someone's struggles
- Exposing private conversations to others
- Using sensitive information to embarrass or hurt

Even if the statement is technically true, truth delivered without compassion becomes verbal harm. What she trusted you with should never become your weapon.

SISTERHOOD ALSO REQUIRES ACCOUNTABILITY

Being emotionally intelligent doesn't mean avoiding the truth. A real friend also offers loving accountability.

She might say: "Sis, I love you. But this situation doesn't look like the woman I know you can be."

That's not criticism. That's care. Sometimes we need someone to hold up a mirror so we can see ourselves clearly. And often the woman holding the mirror has also had one held up for her. That is how real growth happens.

REAL VULNERABILITY VS. TRAUMA BONDING

There is a difference between healthy vulnerability and trauma bonding. Trauma bonding happens when a relationship is built only on chaos, venting, and shared pain, with no movement toward healing. Healthy vulnerability means sharing honestly while still inviting growth, reflection, and change.

Sisterhood is not just about unloading pain. It's about helping one another move through it.

REFLECTION QUESTIONS

Have I ever used a friend's vulnerability against her, even in my thoughts?

____

____

When someone shares something painful with me, do I respond with empathy or judgment?

____

Do my friendships feel emotionally safe for honesty?

____

Am I willing to lovingly challenge a friend when she's out of alignment and allow her to challenge me, too?

____

If our friendship ended today, could I still be trusted with what I know?

____

SCRIPTURE

"Love prospers when a fault is forgiven, but dwelling on it separates close friends."

Proverbs 17:9 (NLT)

Love protects. Love forgives. Love does not store someone's pain as future ammunition.

WORDS TO REMEMBER

"True sisterhood is when someone tells you the truth you didn't want to hear, but you still feel loved afterward."

Some of the most sacred moments in friendship are the ones no one else ever sees. Not the photos. Not the celebrations. Not the vacations.

But the quiet moments:

The late-night calls.
The tearful confessions.
The painful truths shared in trust.

Those are the moments where sisterhood is truly tested. Her pain is not your weapon. Her secrets are not your gossip. Her healing journey is not your story to tell. Hold her with love. Correct her with grace. Be the mirror she needs, just as you would want someone to do for you.

That is Girl Code.

CHAPTER 9:

CODE OF SAFE SPACE: BE A SISTER, NOT A SPECTATOR

The Rule: Don't watch your sister struggle from the sidelines; create space where she can be honest.

Every woman deserves a friend who notices the pain she doesn't say out loud. This chapter is for the women who have been the support system for everyone else but rarely had someone checking on them. The women who recognize silent cries because they've sent them too. True sisterhood means learning how to recognize those quiet signals and respond with compassion, patience, and wisdom. It means loving your friends through difficult seasons without enabling them, abandoning them, or trying to control the outcome.

LET'S DEFINE: SILENT CRIES FOR HELP

Silent cries are the subtle signals that something isn't right. They don't always sound like "I'm not okay."

Sometimes they look like:

- one-word replies
- cancelled plans
- sudden isolation
- constant exhaustion
- overworking or overperforming

Silent cries rarely scream. They whisper.

SILENT CRIES FROM FRIENDS WITH CHILDREN

Sometimes motherhood hides exhaustion behind a brave face.

You might notice things like:

- She stops posting about her family or children
- Her home feels more chaotic than usual
- She shrugs instead of sharing what's bothering her
- She loses patience more easily
- She always helps others but rejects help for herself
- When she finally gets free time, she spends it sleeping or withdrawing

Support might look like:

- Bringing a meal and disposable plates
- Letting her vent without interrupting
- Taking the kids for a few hours so she can breathe
- Helping clean without making her feel judged
- Reminding her she is more than a mother—she is a whole person

SILENT CRIES FROM FRIENDS WITHOUT CHILDREN

Pain doesn't only show up in busy homes. It can also show up in quiet lives.

Signs might include:

- She says she's "fine," but her energy feels off
- She's suddenly always "too busy" to connect
- She deflects when asked how she's really doing

- She works constantly but never rests
- She jokes about disappearing or starting over
- Her appearance, energy, or habits change noticeably

Support might look like:

- Asking about her spirit, not just her schedule
- Planning meaningful, restorative outings
- Letting her cry without rushing the moment
- Encouraging therapy, journaling, or emotional support

SIGNS SHE MAY BE SUFFERING IN SILENCE

Pay attention when you notice:

- She's present physically but emotionally distant
- Her sleeping habits drastically changed
- She isolates more than usual
- Her tone becomes dry, sarcastic, or withdrawn
- She pulls away from people who love her
- Her spiritual life seems disconnected

Not everyone wants to talk right away. A safe space doesn't force vulnerability. It earns it through consistency and care.

SCRIPTURES

"Carry each other's burdens, and in this way you will fulfill the law of Christ."

Galatians 6:2 (NIV)

"Rejoice with those who rejoice; mourn with those who mourn."

Romans 12:15 (ESV)

Sisterhood means meeting someone where they are emotionally. When she celebrates, celebrate. When she cries, sit beside her.

WHEN SILENCE IS SACRED

"When Job's friends heard about all the troubles that had come upon him... they began to weep aloud... Then they sat with him on the ground seven days and seven nights. No one said a word to him, because they saw how great his suffering was."

Job 2:11–13 (NIV)

Pause for a moment and notice what they did. They didn't rush to offer advice. They didn't fill the silence with clichés. They didn't try to fix his pain. They simply sat with him.

Sometimes the most powerful support isn't words. It's presence. Safe spaces aren't loud. They're steady. They aren't full of answers. They're full of availability.

Wisdom to remember: When you don't know what to say, show up and say nothing.

PRAY FOR HER, EVEN WHEN SHE CAN'T PRAY

Sometimes your role isn't to fix the problem. Sometimes your role is simply to cover her. Pray for her peace. Pray for her healing. Pray for her strength to ask for help. And when she finally does? Receive her vulnerability with grace. Never use it against her later. That isn't love. That's control.

BRINGING IT FULL CIRCLE

Sisterhood is not watching your friend struggle while hoping she figures it out alone. It's stepping closer with wisdom, gentleness, and prayer.

Too many women are drowning in silence because no one paused long enough to ask the right question. Or stayed long enough to hear the real answer. We live in a culture that praises women for being "strong" and "low maintenance."

But real safe spaces say something different:

"You don't have to be strong here."
"You don't have to pretend here."
"You don't have to heal alone."

Love is not passive. Love is intentional. And sometimes the greatest act of love is simply being present.

REFLECTION QUESTIONS

Who are the women I check on, but not deeply?

____

____

Have I mistaken someone's silence for strength?

____

____

How can I become a true safe space instead of just a familiar face?

____

____

Do my friends feel emotionally safe with me?

____

When I sense something is wrong, do I lean in or pull away?

____

PRAYER FOR THE SAFE SPACES WE'RE BUILDING

Lord, make me a soft place to land for the women in my life. Give me wisdom to recognize silent cries, courage to respond with compassion, and the patience to sit with someone in their pain. Help me hold space the way You hold space for us, with truth, grace, and unconditional love. Amen.

CHAPTER 10:

CODE OF CONSISTENCY: SHOW UP WHEN IT'S BORING

The Rule: Sisterhood is not seasonal.

THE HEART OF THIS CODE

Not every season is exciting. Not every season is spotlight-worthy. But every season deserves support.

Real friendship isn't only about celebrating wins, sharing highlights, or posting pictures together. Sometimes love looks like showing up when life feels ordinary. Consistency is what turns casual friendships into sacred ones.

THE HONEYMOON PHASE AND WHAT COMES AFTER

Most relationships begin with a honeymoon phase. That stretch where everything feels effortless and exciting. You're texting every day. Laughing constantly. Sending memes. Staying up late talking about life.

But eventually, real life settles in. The conversations slow down. The updates aren't dramatic anymore. Nothing is wrong, but nothing feels exciting either. And this is where consistency gets tested. This is where sisterhood becomes either seasonal or sacred.

THE QUIET SEASONS

Some seasons are simply about surviving:

- Work.
- Bills.
- Children.
- Appointments.
- Daily responsibilities.

You're not socializing, you're sustaining. You're not celebrating, you're maintaining. And that's not disconnection. That's adulthood. In those seasons, no one needs a three-hour conversation.

Sometimes what matters most is a simple message:

"Thinking about you."
"Do you need anything this week?"
"Just sending you love."

These may seem like small gestures. But they are sacred ones.

DIFFERENT FRIENDS, DIFFERENT RHYTHMS

Not every friend moves at the same pace, and that's okay.

You may have:

- The dream chaser who is always building something
- The introvert who restores herself in quiet
- The caregiver whose life revolves around others
- The friend who mirrors your energy and understands when you go quiet

Consistency doesn't mean constant conversation. It means continued connection. Love adjusts its rhythm without disappearing.

THE FRIENDS WHO GET OVERLOOKED

Some women appear distant, but the truth is they are simply stretched thin. They're not dry, they're drained. They're not flaky, they're plates full. Their lives are filled with responsibilities that leave little room for noise. And these are often the friends who need support the most. Show up for the ones who don't always ask. Show up for the ones who don't always speak. Show up even when nothing seems to be happening. That is real sisterhood.

BORING DOESN'T MEAN BROKEN

Some friendships don't end. They simply flatten for a season. That doesn't mean they are failing. It means they are real. Not every call will be deep. Not every message will be long. Not every season will be loud. But the quiet seasons are where trust grows stronger. Friendship isn't only built in celebration. It's built in the slow, steady, ordinary moments in between.

SCRIPTURE

"A friend loves at all times, and a brother is born for a time of adversity."

Proverbs 17:17 (NIV)

NOTICE THE WORDS, AT ALL TIMES.

Not only when life is exciting. Not only when someone is thriving. Love remains steady even when life feels uneventful.

REFLECTION QUESTIONS

Have I ever drifted from a friendship simply because things became quiet or routine?

Do I sometimes mistake someone's peaceful life for being "boring"?

How can I intentionally show love to a friend who may be in a slow or demanding season?

REAL TALK

Show up when life slows down. Show up when she hasn't posted in a while. Show up when she's simply trying to get through the week. Because friendships are not hobbies. They are lifelines.

Real sisterhood is not built in the highlight moments. It is strengthened in the stillness. And sometimes the most meaningful act of love is simply showing up when nothing exciting is happening.

CHAPTER 11:

CODE OF HEALING: DO THE INNER WORK SO YOU CAN BE A
SAFE WOMAN

The Rule: Heal so your presence becomes medicine, not poison.

Some women crave sisterhood. Some women are afraid of it. And some women unknowingly sabotage it.

This chapter is for the women:

- who have done healing work but still struggle to trust
- who want deeper friendships but don't know how to build them
- who were never taught how to love, only how to survive

You cannot fully live by Girl Code if your soul is still leaking from unhealed wounds. You cannot celebrate another woman if your heart is still competing. You cannot be someone's lifeline if you are drowning in your own pain. Healing is not optional. It is foundational.

WHAT ARE MAMA WOUNDS?

"Mama wounds" are the emotional injuries left behind by mothers or mother figures who were:

- emotionally unavailable
- overly critical
- controlling
- distant
- absent (emotionally, physically, or spiritually)

When tenderness wasn't modeled, emotional safety was never learned. Instead of learning how to receive love, many women learned how to anticipate harm.

SIGNS YOU MAY BE CARRYING MAMA WOUNDS

You may notice patterns such as:

- Affection feels uncomfortable or suspicious
- You shut down when women try to get close
- You trust men more easily than women, even when men have hurt you
- Compliments or celebrations make you uncomfortable
- You tend to "mother" everyone instead of being vulnerable
- You isolate when emotional conversations deepen
- You believe love must be earned, performed, or repaid

These patterns are not personality traits. They are protective responses formed from past experiences.

THE LIE WE OFTEN TELL

You've probably heard these phrases before, maybe even said some yourself:

"I don't deal with women."
"Women are too messy."
"I get along better with men."

But most of the time, that statement isn't personality. It's pain.

Often, what it really means is:

- "I've been betrayed by women before."
- "I don't feel emotionally safe around women."
- "I don't know how to handle softness, so I avoid it."

If love was not modeled in safe ways growing up, closeness can feel unfamiliar or even threatening.

WHEN LOVE FEELS FOREIGN

I had a friend growing up who expressed affection freely. She hugged me. She kissed my cheek. She told me she loved me every time we saw each other. And every time, part of me froze. Not because I didn't appreciate her. But because I had never experienced love like that before.

In my home, there were no hugs. No "I love you." No emotional conversations. Just survival. So when my friend offered love so openly, I didn't know what to do with it. I sometimes hugged her back. But I could rarely say the words. Not because I didn't feel love. But because I didn't understand it yet. Later, as I began healing, I realized something powerful: She was offering me the kind of love I had always needed. I just wasn't ready to receive it at the time.

HEALING IS THE DOORWAY TO SAFE WOMANHOOD

It's difficult to love your friends well when:

- You don't trust love
- You mistake kindness for manipulation
- You fear vulnerability

Softness cannot be performed. It grows from healing.

The healed woman does not:

- compete with other women
- gossip to feel powerful
- flinch when someone shows care
- confuse love with control

She has walked through fire. But she comes out warm now, not burned anymore.

SCRIPTURE: THE BLUEPRINT FOR FRIENDSHIP

"A friend loves at all times, and a sister is born for adversity."

Proverbs 17:17 (NIV)

Friendship is not meant to exist only in easy seasons.

It shows up:

- when things are uncomfortable
- when things are quiet
- when someone is struggling
- when someone feels distant

Real sisterhood is not a highlight reel. It is both a mirror and a refuge.

A real friend doesn't say, "Why are you like this?"
She says, "I see you. And I'm still here."

REFLECTION QUESTIONS

In what ways have I unintentionally been unsafe for other women?

____

What parts of me still flinch when love gets close?

____

What healing work might God be inviting me to begin?

____

____

Awareness is often the first step toward transformation.

HEALING AFFIRMATIONS

Speak these words over yourself:

I am the friend who loves with honesty and grace.
I am the sister who shows up in difficult seasons.
My presence creates safety, not fear.
I give the love I once needed, and I give it freely.
God is softening the places life once hardened.

FULL-CIRCLE FOR ME

Healing changed me. It transformed me into the woman I once ran from. The soft one. The honest one. The affectionate one. The whole one. That woman used to scare me. Now I am her. And because of that, I can love another woman without fear, comparison, or control. That is the power of healing. And that is what safe womanhood looks like.

CHAPTER 12:

CODE OF SEXUAL RESPECT: DON'T TOUCH WHAT WAS HERS

The Rule: Her past, present, and private life are off-limits. period, unless she shares it.

WHAT'S ALWAYS OFF-LIMITS

Some boundaries in sisterhood should never need explanation. They simply exist because respect exists.

That includes:

Her Man: If she is with him, whether publicly, privately, long-distance, spiritually, or common-law, he is hers. Respect that.

Her Ex: If he once had access to her heart, her body, or her tears, he is not yours to explore.

Her Situationship: Titles don't erase emotional history. If she once loved him, claimed him, or cried over him, you know better.

Her Family: Her brother, cousin, uncle, and family members. If you ever find yourself interested in someone connected to your friend, have the maturity to discuss it first, not after. Some doors simply require respect before curiosity.

When one woman betrays another over a man, it is rarely about the man.

It is about something deeper:

The sacredness of what was shared between you.
The safety she believed she had with you.
Because you didn't just cross a romantic boundary, you crossed a friendship boundary.
And what hurts most is not the relationship; it is the betrayal of trust.

WHY WOMEN SOMETIMES MAKE EXCUSES

When this boundary is crossed, the explanations often sound familiar:

"It just happened."
"Y'all weren't even together anymore."
"I didn't think you cared about him like that."

But these explanations usually reveal something deeper:

Selfishness disguised as justification.
Friendship is not built on technicalities.
It is built on trust.

THE AFTERMATH

Some friendships try to move forward after this kind of betrayal. But many never truly recover. Not because forgiveness is impossible. But because trust, once broken in this way, rarely returns to what it was.

What often replaces it is:

Silent tension
Subtle competition
Unspoken resentment
Emotional distance

Sometimes the friendship survives on the surface. But underneath, something sacred has shifted.

REAL TALK

You should never desire what your sister has loved, touched, or grieved over. Not her man. Not her money. Not her momentum.

Admire her, yes.
Learn from her, yes.

But comparison can quietly distort admiration. And comparison is often where envy begins.

REDEMPTION IS POSSIBLE, BUT IT REQUIRES HONESTY

If you are the one who crossed the boundary:

Apologize without defending yourself.
Accept the consequences of the hurt you caused.
Do not rush her healing or try to pretend things are "normal."
Respect the space she may need.

If you are the one who was betrayed:

You do not owe anyone quick forgiveness, but you do deserve closure, clarity, and peace.
Protecting your heart is not bitterness; it is wisdom.

SCRIPTURE

"For where you have envy and selfish ambition, there you find disorder and every evil practice."

James 3:16

Envy does not always appear loudly.

Sometimes it shows up quietly as:

Backhanded compliments
Subtle comparisons
Curiosity about what someone else has
Silent satisfaction when someone falls

Long before someone crosses a physical boundary, envy has already crossed an emotional one.

REFLECTION QUESTIONS

Do I carry silent comparisons toward any of my friends?

____

____

Have I ever admired something about another woman to the point of resentment or obsession?

____

Have I ever minimized someone's pain to justify my own choices?

Can I hold myself accountable without needing someone else's forgiveness to feel better?

Do I need to release guilt, resentment, or unresolved hurt tied to a broken boundary?

Sexual respect in sisterhood is about far more than relationships. It is about boundaries. It is about honoring another woman's experiences, heartbreaks, and healing. It is understood that some things are not yours, not because you cannot have them, but because your character will not allow you to take them.

Real sisters move with respect. Not secrecy. Not competition. Not betrayal. And anything that costs you your character is never worth the curiosity.

You didn't just cross a line with him. You crossed a line with her. And that kind of betrayal not only breaks trust, it also breaks sisterhood.

CHAPTER 13:

CODE OF CONNECTION: HER PEOPLE ARE YOUR PEOPLE

The Rule: If y'all are locked in, her family matters too.

SISTERHOOD EXTENDS BEYOND THE FRIENDSHIP

Sisterhood doesn't stop at brunch dates, matching nails, or late-night vent sessions. When you are truly locked in with someone, your connection extends beyond just the two of you. Her world becomes part of your world. Her children should know your name, not just your Instagram handle. Her mother, cousins, siblings, and close circle are not strangers. They are extensions of the woman you love and call sister. Real sisterhood grows roots, and roots reach into the family.

WHY FAMILY MATTERS IN FRIENDSHIP

For many women, friendship becomes the closest thing to family. Especially for women who have had to distance themselves from their own families for unhealthy reasons. Sometimes your friend's family becomes a space where you experience pieces of the wholeness you were missing. Their little quirks or dysfunctions may not scare you. As long as they are not harming your sister, you can embrace them with grace. But sometimes family members may question your presence.

You may hear comments like:

"Why are you always around?"
"What do you want with my cousin?"
"Y'all act like sisters now."

Don't take those moments personally. Often, those comments are not about you. They are simply people trying to understand a love they didn't expect or haven't experienced themselves.

NAVIGATING HER CIRCLE

When you are around her family, remember:

You represent loyalty.
You represent respect.
You represent the friendship she trusts.

You don't have to force yourself to fit in. Just show up with kindness and integrity. If someone behaves disrespectfully or inappropriately within the family dynamic, address it with maturity, not gossip. Speak with grace. Protect the peace of the environment you've been welcomed into.

WHEN CHILDREN ARE PART OF THE PICTURE

When children are involved, the connection grows even deeper. Her children may begin to see you as another safe adult in their lives. Your children may grow alongside hers.

Suddenly the friendship expands into something bigger:

Extra aunts
Extra cousins
Extra support systems

These bonds do not happen overnight. They grow through time, trust, and consistent presence. Chosen family is built slowly. But when it forms, it becomes powerful.

THE POWER OF SHOWING UP

Women often feel love through presence. Showing up does not mean spending money or doing something extravagant. It simply means making space. You planned. You scheduled. You prioritized being there.

Moments that matter include:

Baby showers
Birthdays
Funerals
Graduations
School events
Family gatherings

These are the seasons where presence speaks louder than words.

Showing up says:
"You matter enough to be woven into my life rhythm."

CONSISTENCY KEEPS THE CONNECTION ALIVE

Think of sisterhood like an extension cord. When it is plugged in, energy flows. When it is frayed or disconnected, the power fades. Connection requires consistent effort. Not constant conversation. But intentional presence.

Small habits help keep the bond alive:

Visit your sister occasionally instead of only texting.
Remember birthdays and important milestones.
Check in during quiet seasons.

Consistency builds emotional safety.

BOUNDARIES AND RECIPROCITY

Connection must always include respect. You are there to support, not replace. Honor her role within her family. Never overstep or insert yourself where you do not belong.

Healthy connection is also mutual. It is not just about you showing up for her family. There should also be care for yours. And if tension ever arises between her and her family, stay grounded. Stand beside her, not between them. Offer support quietly. Avoid becoming a voice that fuels division. Sometimes prayer and presence are more powerful than opinions.

TALK ABOUT IT WHEN SOMETHING FEELS OFF

Sometimes hurt feelings come from unspoken expectations. Maybe your friend didn't show up in the way you hoped. Maybe you felt overlooked or unsupported. Instead of carrying silent resentment, talk about it. Honest conversations prevent small misunderstandings from becoming lasting distance. Silence can build walls. Communication builds understanding.

When was the last time I showed up for my sister outside of convenience?

____

____

Do her family members know me personally, or only through social media?

____

____

Have I ever taken offense to her family's reactions when it may have simply been unfamiliarity?

____

____

What is one consistent way I can reconnect with my sisterhood bond this month?

____

____

When my sister cannot show up for me, do I respond with grace or resentment?

____

____

Am I covering her family in prayer as much as I support her?

____

____

"Two are better than one... If either of them falls, one can help the other up."

Ecclesiastes 4:9–10

Life was never meant to be carried alone. Support multiplies strength.

BRINGING IT FULL CIRCLE

Sisterhood is about presence, but it is also about placement. Know your role in her world and honor it with humility. Love her family. Respect her roots. Protect her peace. But always remember: she is the bridge that connects you all.

You are not there to replace anyone. You are there to expand the love. Showing up is not just about attendance. It is about alignment.

It says: "I see you. I value you. I'm walking through life with you."

Because connection without consistency fades. And support without respect fractures. But when sisterhood is built on trust, time, and tenderness, something beautiful happens. Real sisterhood does more than connect women. It connects legacies.

CHAPTER 14:

CODE OF DISCERNMENT: HELP HER, DON'T HIJACK HER HEALING

The Rule: You are her sister, not her savior.

This one goes deep. Because for many of us, helping isn't just something we do. It's who we've always been. We've carried. We've fixed. We've poured. We've rescued. Until helping became our identity. But if we're honest, some of that instinct didn't come from strength. It came from unhealed wounds.

Sometimes we became the mothers we never had, overextending ourselves, confusing compassion with control, and calling it love. We poured until we were empty. We mistook exhaustion for loyalty.

But here's the truth:

You can guide her, but you cannot grow her. You can hand her tools, but you cannot swing the hammer for her. There is a fine line between helping and hijacking. And sometimes we cross it because being needed feels like being valued.

THE MOMMY ROLE

Many friendships quietly fall into a pattern of emotional parenting. One woman needs to be mothered. Another feels compelled to mother. What begins as nurturing can slowly turn into dependency. You become her emotional home. Her counselor. Her comfort. Her safety net. And before long, you are carrying burdens that were never yours.

When you play the role of "mama," something important gets lost. You rob her of accountability. And you rob yourself of peace. Even good intentions can interrupt God's lesson plan.

SELF-CHECK

Take a moment to ask yourself honestly:

- Am I offering guidance, or am I competing with God?

- Do I trust her enough to let her fall and find her footing?

- Have I made her my project instead of my peer?

- Is my help Spirit-led, or ego-fed?

When love starts sounding like control, or care turns into resentment, something is out of alignment. That's not discernment. That's a sign it's time to step back.

UNDERSTANDING THE DIFFERENCE

There is a difference between pity, empathy, and discernment.

Pity says, "I feel sorry for you."
Empathy says, "I understand what you're feeling, and I'll stand beside you."
Discernment says, "I love you enough to trust God with your process."

We are all called to care. But we are not called to carry everything. There is a holy balance between being a sister and trying to be someone's savior.

SCRIPTURE

"Cast your cares on the Lord and He will sustain you."

Psalm 55:22

This verse reminds us of something essential:

You are not the sustainer. God is.

You can pray. You can encourage. You can support. But you cannot replace the work God is doing in someone else's life. True love doesn't take over. It trusts enough to let go.

TESTIMONY: WHEN HELPING HURT ME

For a long time, I believed being the strong friend was my purpose. I mothered grown women because, deep down, I still needed a mother myself. I showed up with food, money, rides, and late-night pep talks. I was the one everyone called when their world fell apart.

And honestly? Part of me loved it. It made me feel needed. Important. Essential. But eventually, I realized something painful. I wasn't helping anymore. I was hand-holding people through healing that wasn't mine. Every time I rushed in to fix something, I delayed what God was trying to teach them. I mistook pity for empathy. I confused rescuing with loving. And one day I looked around and realized I was empty. I had poured so much into everyone else that I barely recognized myself.

That's when the truth hit me:

Being everyone's mother left no room for me to simply be God's daughter. When I finally stepped back, it was uncomfortable. Some people were upset. Some friendships changed, a few even ended. But something else walked in the moment I created space. Peace. I learned that boundaries are not betrayal. They are obedience.

Now I remind myself daily:

You are her sister.
Not her savior.
My job isn't to carry her life.
My job is to pray for her, encourage her, and trust God to sustain her where I cannot.

REFLECTION PROMPTS

Am I helping her heal, or holding her hostage to my help?

____

Do I mother my friends because of my own unhealed wounds?

____

Have I mistaken pity for empathy?

____

Have I stepped into God's role without realizing it?

____

If I step back, do I trust that God will sustain her where I cannot?

Growth begins with awareness. Remember: "You can't carry her cross. You can only help her keep walking toward resurrection."

PRAYER

Lord, give me the wisdom to discern the difference between helping and hindering. Teach me to love my sisters through You, not instead of You. Remind me that You alone are the healer, the sustainer, and the savior. Help my hands release what my heart tries to hold. In Jesus' name, Amen.

CHAPTER 15:

CODE OF LOYALTY: STOP STRADDLING THE FENCE

The Rule: If you're neutral in conflict, you've already chosen a side, and it's not hers.

WHERE FENCE-SITTING SHOWS UP

Sometimes disloyalty doesn't look loud. It looks comfortable.

You see it in:

Friend groups: Watching gossip fly while saying nothing to correct the lie.

Work environments: Laughing with leadership while your sister gets overlooked or treated unfairly.

Family dynamics: Excusing toxic relatives with "that's just how they are."

Social circles with shared history: Entertaining both sides of old drama while claiming, "I don't get involved."

But loyalty requires more than observation. It requires integrity.

WHY NEUTRALITY ISN'T NEUTRAL

Neutrality often feels peaceful. But most of the time, it is simply avoidance. Neutrality protects comfort, not truth. Silence can feel safe in the moment. But over time, silence breeds betrayal. Because when wrong behavior is protected, it continues. And when truth is ignored, trust begins to erode.

As the saying goes, "You can't sit at my table and serve them tea."

If someone is harming your sister while you quietly entertain both sides, the message becomes clear: Comfort matters more than loyalty.

THE BROKENNESS TRAP

Unhealed people often defend unhealthy behavior. Not because it's right. But because it feels familiar. When dysfunction becomes normal, people begin to protect it.

You'll often hear phrases like:

"That's just how she is."
"She didn't mean it like that."
"She's just having a bad day."
"You know she's been through a lot."

But empathy should never silence accountability. Understanding someone's pain does not excuse their harmful behavior. Truth and compassion can exist at the same time.

DEFINING LOYALTY AND ALIGNMENT

Loyalty: A faithful commitment to truth, integrity, and love.

Loyalty does not mean defending someone's wrong behavior. It means standing firmly for what is right.

Alignment: When your values, words, and actions match.

When you are aligned, you stop negotiating with dysfunction. You move with clarity instead of confusion. If someone remains aligned with chaos, their loyalty will eventually follow that chaos, not you.

THE COST OF SILENCE

When women stay quiet to keep the peace, something sacred is lost:

Trust, the hurt sister, begins to question whether you would protect her.
Integrity, your credibility weakens because your actions don't match your values.
Peace, you feel internal conflict trying to please everyone.

Neutrality is never free. Every time you choose comfort over truth, integrity pays the price.

LOYALTY WITH DISCERNMENT

True loyalty is not blind. It is honest. Loyalty does not mean standing behind someone's mistakes. It means standing beside them in truth.

If you love her:

You will correct her privately.
You will encourage growth.
You will refuse to support behavior that harms others.

And if she rejects accountability? You step back with grace. Loyalty never requires you to participate in dysfunction.

SCRIPTURE

"Remember, it is sin to know what you ought to do and then not do it."

James 4:17

Sometimes silence is not wisdom. Sometimes silence is avoidance. Knowing the right thing but refusing to act is still a choice.

REFLECTION QUESTIONS

Have I ever stayed silent when my sister needed me to speak up?

____

Was my silence rooted in fear, comfort, or convenience?

____

Am I aligned with truth in my friendships, or protecting comfort instead?

____

What does loyalty look like in my life (protection, presence, or correction)?

____

____

Honest answers lead to growth.

Walking Away Without Guilt

Sometimes the hardest act of loyalty is recognizing when alignment no longer exists. Walking away does not mean you stopped caring. It means you chose peace over chaos.

Here are ways to step back with integrity:

1. Acknowledge the Misalignment: Be honest when your values no longer match the environment around you.
2. Release the Role: You cannot fix what does not want to heal.
3. Set Boundaries: Wish her well, but protect your peace.
4. Forgive Quietly: Forgiveness frees your heart. Reconciliation is not always required.
5. Pray and Detach: Ask God to handle what your words cannot reach.

Leaving a toxic environment does not mean you have stopped loving someone. It means you finally started loving yourself again.

THE TRUTH ABOUT LOYALTY

Loyalty without truth becomes captivity. Alignment without courage becomes performance. You were never called to live in the middle of the fence. You were called to be light. And light does not hide. Even when it costs comfort. Even when it costs company. Even when it costs connection. Because real loyalty does not straddle fences.

It builds bridges where truth can cross.

FULL CIRCLE

THE LEGACY OF THE GIRL CODE

The Rule: Be the woman who teaches with love, corrects with grace, and leads with light.

Fifteen chapters later, you've walked through conversations most women are too afraid to say out loud.

Together we explored:

Loyalty.
Presence.
Boundaries.
Respect.
Accountability.
Healing.
Growth.

You've reflected on what it truly means to be your sister's keeper, not only when it's easy, but when it's uncomfortable, inconvenient, or convicting.

The Girl Code was never written for perfection. It was written for progression. For women who have been broken but still choose to build. For women who have been betrayed but still choose to believe in sisterhood. For women who love deeply but are learning how to love wisely.

These codes are more than words. They are principles. A reminder that authentic womanhood is sacred, not performative. And when women honor each other through respect, honesty, and accountability, something powerful happens. We create a sisterhood that cannot be canceled, copied, or corrupted.

THE MESSAGE: PROTECT THE CIRCLE

As you step away from these pages, remember what sustains true sisterhood:

Confidentiality sustains it.
Accountability strengthens it.
Boundaries protect it.
Grace restores it.
Growth expands it.
Emotional intelligence purifies it.
Safe spaces heal it.
Connection extends it.
Sexual respect honors it.
Sisterhood depends on all of it.

The legacy of the Girl Code is not simply to read these principles. It is to live them. Because sisterhood is not a title. It is a way of life.

SCRIPTURE TO SEAL THE CIRCLE

"She opens her mouth with wisdom, and the teaching of kindness is on her tongue."

Proverbs 31:26

May we be women who speak with wisdom. Women who teach kindness. Women who walk boldly in the grace and strength God designed us to carry. Because when one woman chooses healing, she changes her circle. When a circle changes, communities change. And when communities change, legacies are rewritten.

That is the power of living the Girl Code.

REFLECTION PROMPTS

Use these questions to turn reflection into action.

1. Presence & Consistency

Where in my friendships have I expected support that I have not consistently offered? Where could I be more present, emotionally or physically?

2. Confidentiality & Trust

Can my sisters trust me with their truth? What does loyalty look like when no one else is watching?

3. Celebration & Comparison

Do I celebrate other women openly, or silently compete in my mind? How can I practice gratitude instead of comparison?

4. Accountability & Grace

When a friend offends me, do I confront the issue or quietly detach? How can I correct her with love instead of shame?

5. Boundaries & Overgiving

Do I give from love or from guilt? What boundaries do I need to rebuild to protect my peace?

6. Emotional Intelligence

When I'm hurt, do I respond thoughtfully or react emotionally? What emotions might I need to sit with instead of projecting onto others?

7. Safe Space & Support

How can I become a safe place for another woman to land? And who in my life can be that safe place for me?

8. Healing & Sisterhood

What wounds from past friendships still affect how I trust women today? What might forgiveness, without restored access, look like in my life?

9. Sexual Respect & Integrity

Do I honor the relationships, families, and boundaries around me? How can my character reflect integrity even in unseen moments?

10. Legacy

What will other women learn about God, love, and healing by watching my life? How can I pass these codes to my daughters, nieces, and the next generation of women?

*If the women closest to me described my friendship, would it reflect the Girl Code I just read?

AUTHOR'S CLOSING NOTE

To every woman who's ever been misunderstood, mishandled, or misloved, this is for you.

To the women who had to become what they never had, this is for you.

And to the women healing from the wounds caused by other women, this is for you, too.

The Girl Code is a reminder that we are not enemies; we are evidence that women can rebuild, relearn, and reconnect without rivalry.

I pray that these codes guide your conversations, friendships, and evolution.

Keep loving.

Keep growing.

Keep choosing alignment over attachment.

And remember, you don't have to fit in when you were chosen to stand out.

Welcome to the circle, sis.

You are now officially Girl Coded.

WITH LOVE,

Eclesia Holmes

GLOSSARY

THE LANGUAGE OF SISTERHOOD

Accountability

The willingness to take responsibility for your actions, words, and behavior while allowing trusted people to correct you in love.

Alignment

The harmony between your values, your words, and your actions. When you are aligned, your life reflects what you claim to believe.

Boundaries

Healthy limits that protect your emotional, spiritual, and mental well-being. Boundaries clarify what behavior you will accept and what you will not.

Celebration

Actively supporting and honoring another woman's success, growth, or happiness without comparison or competition.

Comparison

Measuring your life against another woman's journey. Comparison distorts admiration and can quietly breed jealousy.

Connection

The intentional effort to build meaningful relationships through presence, consistency, and shared life experiences.

Confidentiality

The sacred commitment to protect what another woman shares with you in vulnerability. Her truth is not gossip material.

GLOSSARY

THE LANGUAGE OF SISTERHOOD

Confrontation

Addressing an issue directly and respectfully rather than avoiding it. Healthy confrontation seeks understanding and growth, not punishment.

Discernment

The spiritual and emotional wisdom to know when to help, when to step back, and when to trust God to work in someone's life.

Emotional Intelligence

The ability to understand, manage, and respond to emotions, your own and others', with awareness, maturity, and compassion.

Empathy

The ability to understand and share another person's feelings while standing beside them in support.

Grace

Offering compassion, patience, and forgiveness even when someone has made a mistake.

Healing

The ongoing process of addressing past wounds so they no longer control your present behavior or relationships.

Integrity

Doing what is right even when it is uncomfortable, unpopular, or unseen.

Jealousy

A feeling of insecurity or resentment that arises when comparing yourself to another person's success, attention, or opportunities.

GLOSSARY

THE LANGUAGE OF SISTERHOOD

Loyalty

A faithful commitment to stand for truth, respect, and integrity in your friendships. Loyalty supports righteousness, not wrongdoing.

Neutrality

Avoiding taking a stand in situations where truth and loyalty require action. Neutrality often protects comfort instead of justice.

People-Pleasing

Betraying your own needs or boundaries in order to gain approval, acceptance, or validation from others.

Safe Space

An environment where someone feels emotionally secure enough to be honest, vulnerable, and authentic without fear of judgment or betrayal.

Sexual Respect

Honoring the romantic and relational boundaries connected to your friends. This includes respecting their partners, ex-partners, and emotional history.

Sisterhood

A supportive bond between women built on trust, respect, accountability, and love.

Support

Providing encouragement, presence, and guidance without taking control of another person's life or responsibilities.

GLOSSARY
THE LANGUAGE OF SISTERHOOD

Trust

The confidence that someone will handle your vulnerability with care and respect.

Vulnerability

The courage to share your authentic feelings, struggles, or experiences with someone you trust.

ABOUT THE AUTHOR

Eclesia Holmes is a writer, mentor, and advocate for healthy sisterhood and personal growth among women.

As the founder of Pen to Purpose Publishing LLC, she is passionate about helping women turn their stories, experiences, and lessons into tools that inspire healing, accountability, and transformation.

Through her writing, Eclesia encourages women to embrace emotional intelligence, set healthy boundaries, and cultivate friendships built on respect, loyalty, and truth. Her work focuses on breaking cycles of comparison and competition while restoring the sacred value of authentic sisterhood.

Girl Code was written as both a guide and a mirror, challenging women to grow, love wisely, and protect the bonds that strengthen communities.

Eclesia believes that when women heal, support one another, and walk in integrity, they create legacies that extend far beyond themselves.

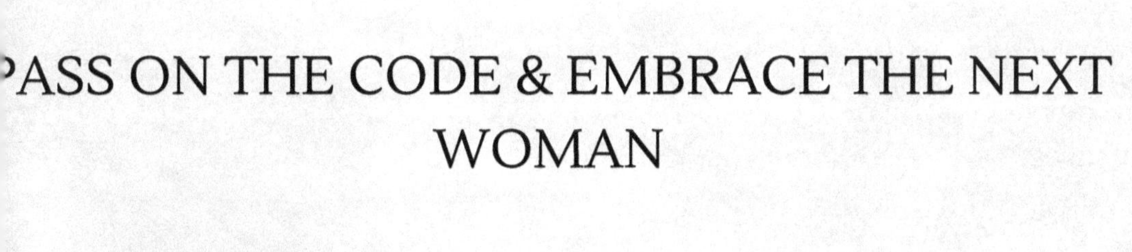

PASS ON THE CODE & EMBRACE THE NEXT
WOMAN